Y0-BZL-206

High School Musicals™

STAGE MANAGEMENT and PRODUCTION

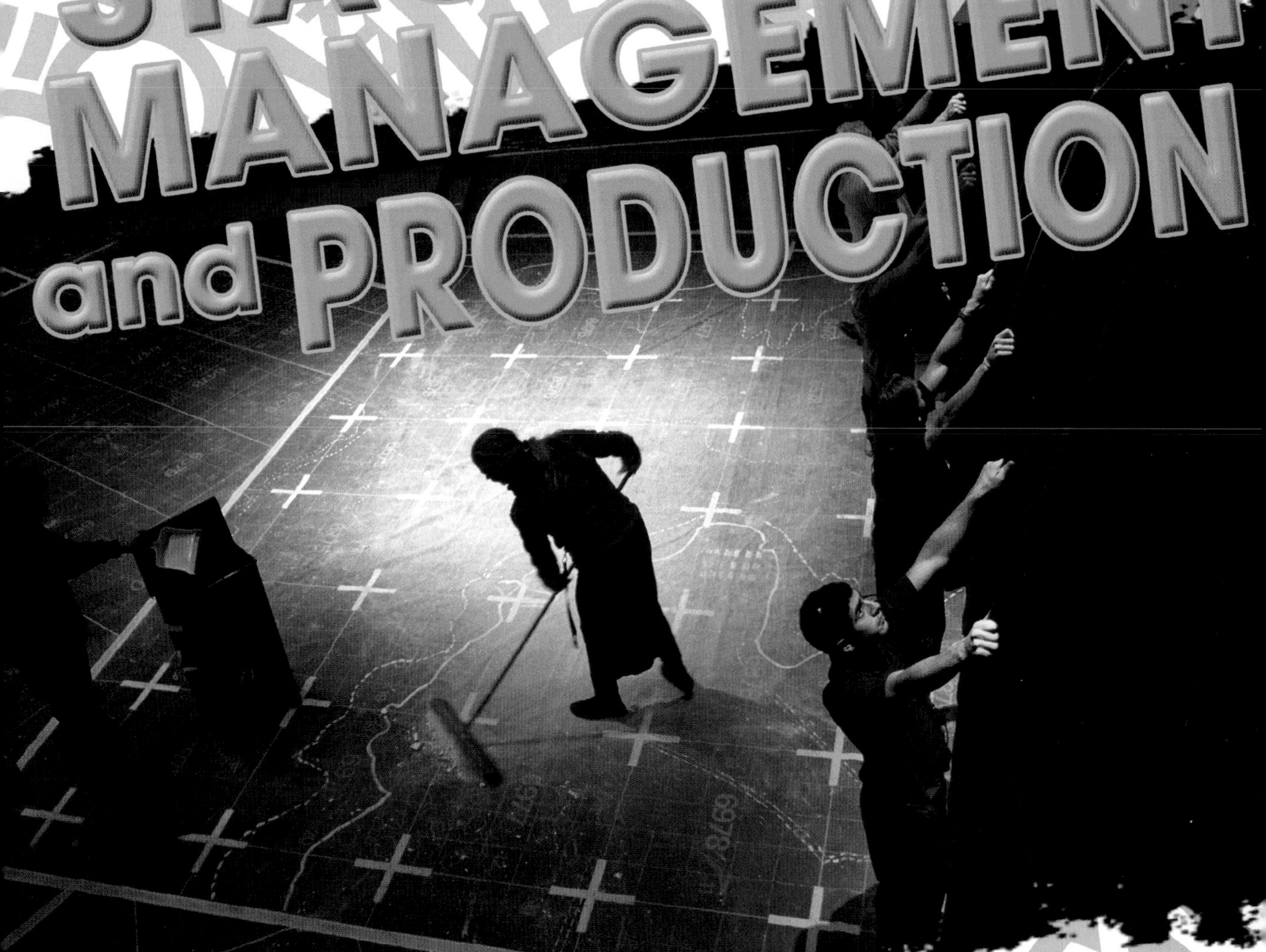

Diane Bailey

rosen publishing's
rosen
central®
New York

Published in 2010 by The Rosen Publishing Group, Inc.
29 East 21st Street, New York, NY 10010

Library of Congress Cataloging-in-Publication Data

Bailey, Diane, 1966–
Stage management and production / Diane Bailey.
   p. cm.—(High school musicals)
Includes bibliographical references and index.
ISBN-13: 978-1-4358-5260-0 (library binding)
ISBN-13: 978-1-4358-5534-2 (pbk)
ISBN-13: 978-1-4358-5535-9 (6 pack)
1. Stage management. 2. Musicals—Production and direction. I. Title.
MT955.B182 2009
792.602'3—dc22

                               2008044020

Manufactured in Malaysia

Contents

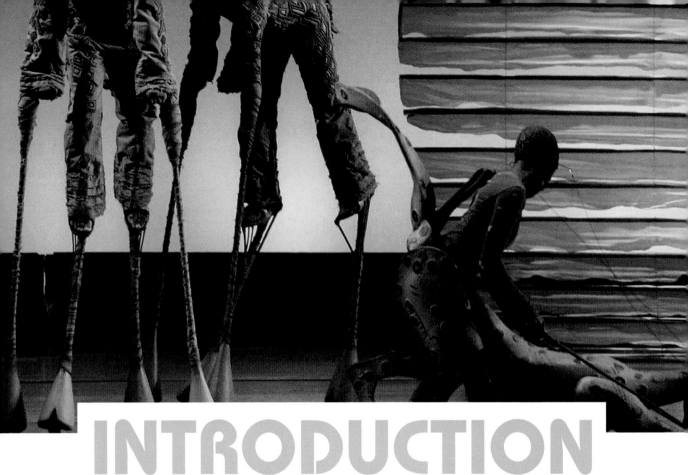

INTRODUCTION

*T*he Lion King had no king. In the musical, there's a struggle over who gets to be king. But backstage at the show, it seemed no one was up to the job, at least for the night. The actor who played Simba was sick and couldn't go onstage. The understudy was sick, too.

But this was a big Broadway show. There was an understudy to the understudy. This actor was new to the show, however, and had not yet played the role. He went onstage to practice a difficult move—and sprained his ankle. Now, he couldn't perform either. The audience was taking its seats, and there was no one to play one of the show's major roles.

Everyone in a show can run into problems. Actors might rip their costumes. The lighting technicians might discover that the

spotlight is burned out. The crew might drop something and break it. But none of those people has to worry about the others.

The stage manager does. Whether it's a ripped costume, a burned-out light, or a broken set, if it can't be fixed by the person who found the problem, it falls to the stage manager. A disaster is officially his problem. The stage manager has got to solve it or cancel the performance.

In the case of *The Lion King*, a stage manager knew of a performance of *Aida* that was happening down the street. One of the actors had been in *The Lion King* a couple of years earlier. (He played a giraffe but covered the role of Simba.) The stage manager called the other theater and explained the problem. Although the actor was already dressed for his part in *Aida*, they

Behind the Stage

That's not my job! Stage managers will never see that line in their scripts. A stage manager is the ultimate go-to guy. Many different jobs go into putting on a show. The stage manager does not do them all. However, he's the one who makes sure they get done. If he notices a problem with the sets or the lighting, he tells the people in those departments. On the professional stage, he will be the one checking the refrigerator to see that there's plenty of the director's favorite kind of soda. And he might be doing the most humble of tasks that falls to the stage manager: sweeping the stage. Yes, with a broom.

What It Takes

The job description of a stage manager is "Do everything." What must that person be like? The answer is probably, "Be everything."

Even stage managers sometimes get a moment in the spotlight while they do one of their basic jobs: sweeping the stage.

A stage manager is like a concierge at a fancy hotel. He knows everyone. He knows what everyone does. And he knows how to get people to do things.

Many stage managers have spent time acting, working the light board, or painting sets. All of these can come in handy when it comes to stage management. It helps to know how the job is done.

Besides having a lot of different skills, a stage manager needs a certain kind of personality. Not everyone has it. "All the classes in the world won't make me a better singer," said stage manager Michele Kay in an article in *Dramatics* magazine. "The same can be said for stage managers."

Stage managers coordinate with crew members to determine where sets and props will be placed onstage during each scene.

A good stage manager must be responsible, organized, and flexible. He should be detail-oriented in order to keep track of the hundreds of little issues that come up during a show. At the same time, a stage manager should not lose sight of the big picture. He should have a good sense of what is really important in order to produce a successful show.

A stage manager should be good at spotting—and solving—problems before they get too big. However, something always goes

The stage manager may consult with the set design and construction crew to make sure that sets and props will not cause any unexpected problems.

wrong—that's pretty much a given in theater! When there is trouble, the stage manager must be able to keep his cool.

Let's suppose the sword used in a battle scene has gotten lost. Hopefully, everyone will keep a clear head and work together to find a solution. However, if there is any panicking, it will have to be done by the actors and the prop people. The stage manager will be too busy to panic. He will be thinking, "We've got to stage a battle scene in two minutes." He might get his trusty broom, break off the handle, and send the actor onstage with a makeshift "sword." Or, he might tell the actors to simply pretend they have weapons. But if he keeps his head, the show will not come to a grinding halt.

The stage manager's kindergarten report card probably said he played well with others. He can deal with all different kinds of personalities. He should always look for solutions that will make people happy, but sometimes his decisions will not be popular. In those cases, he can't be afraid to take a stand.

What makes the perfect stage manager? According to one article on UpstageReview.org, a person should be "more organized than the Library of Congress, have the counseling skills of Dr. Joyce Brothers, the patience of Job, the tact under pressure of Mother Theresa PLUS Dr. Martin Luther King Jr., and be a candidate for sainthood upon retirement."

The Nerve Center

What does a stage manager actually do? That question has a simple answer: whatever has to be done. He makes sure that everyone, from the actors to the stage crew, has what they need. A stage manager is the nerve center of a show. All information goes through him.

A stage manager's job is different with every show. For example, it will depend on how complex the musical is and where it is being staged. In high school, a stage manager's main job probably will be "calling the show." This means making sure that the technical parts

If actors need to change costumes in a hurry, the stage manager will need to set up a quick-change area near the stage.

of a show—such as light and sound effects—happen at the right time. A high school stage manager might also help at rehearsals and get the backstage area ready for the show. He may work with the people building sets or designing costumes.

Stage managers can be highly creative people. However, their job is to help the other creative people. Unless he is asked, the stage manager usually keeps his opinions to himself. Sometimes,

It may look like just a jumble of stuff, but the stage manager will figure out where to store sets and props so that the crew can get to them easily.

he might see that something is going to cause a safety risk. Or, there might be a huge technical problem. Then, he can—and should—speak up. In general, though, if the idea is workable, he should work with it—even if he doesn't like it.

If you are interested in a career in stage management, ask the director about ways you can become involved. Then, you can learn more about how all the parts of the show work together.

Stage managers are sometimes called "the director's shadow." They usually work closely with the director. The stage manager takes the pressure off the director. He takes notes about what happens in rehearsal. What went wrong and needs attention? He troubleshoots problems that would take up the director's time. He makes sure the cast and crew know what the director wants. If people have questions, they ask the stage manager first. If he doesn't know the answer, he finds it. He may say, "I don't know," but that's always followed by, "I'll find out."

According to one article on WiseGeek.com about the duties of a stage manager, "Ideally, a stage manager should be the most visible person backstage and the most invisible person onstage."

This means that when a stage manager does his job well, the show runs smoothly. Even if there are problems, the audience won't know it.

Setting the Tone

Although the stage manager is the nerve center of the operation, he can't be the nervous center.

The stage manager sets the tone for the show. His influence is felt every day. In professional theater, the director often leaves the show after opening night. He created the show, and his job is

Who's My Boss?

In professional theater, the boss of a show is the producer. This person is in charge of getting enough money to put on the show. The director works under the producer. Usually, though, the producer won't tell the director how to do his job. (There have been some spectacular fights when this happens!) High school shows usually don't have producers. The director is in charge.

The stage manager works under the director. In some shows, the stage manager is considered an assistant director. A lot of it depends on personalities and how the director and stage manager get along.

Many people work on lighting, sound, costumes, and special effects. They all report to the technical director. The technical director and the stage manager have different responsibilities. However, they will usually work together closely.

A company manager takes care of the business issues with the people working on the show. He makes sure that the actors get paid, for example.

finished. It is the stage manager who keeps it going. He stays until the end. The best stage managers make everyone around them comfortable. They keep a good attitude, deal with people fairly, and follow through on what they say they are going to do.

The stage manager should try to be on good terms with everyone in the cast and crew. This doesn't mean that they all have to be the best of friends. However, their relationships should be friendly, with respect on both sides. The stage manager should be able to depend on the company, and vice versa. That's how everyone will survive the stress of putting on a major show.

The stage manager also helps keep relationships good between other members of the cast and crew. There will undoubtedly be disagreements about how to do things. There may be not-so-friendly competition among the performers. People are working in close quarters and for long hours. It becomes easy to gossip or gang up on certain people. A stage manager should not join any talk or activity that hurts someone else. In fact, he should try to stop it if it does happen.

As stage manager, you may not know how to solve a problem between other people. Or, you may try, but it still continues. In that case, you should go to the director or another adult involved with the show.

Other Responsibilities

Big Broadway musicals have huge staffs. For example, there is an entire department devoted to publicizing the show. Other people are in charge of managing the theater itself. There are people who sell tickets, people who sell food and drinks at intermission, and people who usher the audience to their seats. The house manager handles the public areas of the theater. The stage manager is in charge of everything backstage.

The stage manager and the house manager work together on one very important piece of business: the start of the show. The stage manager must let the house manager know when the show is going to start. He'll report any delays related to the show. If an actor is late or a spotlight needs to be changed at the last minute, the stage manager will tell the house manager. The house manager keeps tabs on other things that might cause a delay. Maybe a snowstorm has caused a huge traffic jam. If the seats are half

In some productions, the stage manager may get involved with other backstage jobs, such as scene-painting.

empty due to circumstances like this, it's a good idea to hold the curtain for a little while, and the house manager tells the stage manager about the change in plans.

In a high school production, the stage manager may also do other jobs related to the show. He may get the school newspaper to write a story about it. He may promote it to the local city paper, too. He can hang up posters, pass out fliers, and make T-shirts. He may get the tickets printed and be in charge of sales.

And if he has time, he might try his hand at painting sets. Probably no one is going to object, as long as he still has time to sweep the stage!

Who's on First?

Pop quiz: Rehearsal starts at 7:00. When should the stage manager get to the theater?

You probably guessed that "7:00" isn't the right answer. Stage managers are usually the first to arrive at rehearsals and the last to leave.

Before the Actors

Now, take this a step further. Stage managers are often among the first people to join the show itself. They usually come on board soon after the director is chosen.

A lot of work goes into a show before the actors ever show up for rehearsal. During pre-production, meetings are held to talk about the design of the show. More meetings are held to talk about scheduling and how much it will cost. A stage manager may go to

During auditions and rehearsals, actors turn to the stage manager when they have questions. The stage manager helps communicate the director's wishes to the actors.

these meetings so that he stays in the loop. He can find out how the decisions will affect his job.

In professional theater, the stage manager also runs the auditions. He schedules the actors' appointments and keeps them moving on time. He does everything calmly and with a smile. This helps nervous performers feel more comfortable. In a high school show, a stage manager may or may not work with the director before rehearsals begin.

When rehearsals do start, the stage manager should find out exactly how the director wants him to be involved. Does the director want him to take notes? Should she talk to the cast or crew about the director's decisions, or would the director prefer to do it himself?

Ask questions if you are confused about anything. The director and the stage manager need to have clear communication. If they

A good stage manager is never without pencil and paper because she's the one in charge of taking notes!

have a misunderstanding, it can trickle down into the rest of the company.

You Are Here

Chances are, you're putting on your musical in the auditorium of

your school. If your school doesn't have a stage, you have probably found a community building or theater. Wherever it is, as stage manager you must know the space inside and out. People will come to you with questions about where things are and how stuff works. It's up to you to have answers.

Professional stage managers work in a new place with every show. They learn everything all over again. As a high school stage manager, you already know your way around the school. So does everyone else in the show. You will not have to point out where the restrooms are.

But now you have to look at the theater more closely. You have to think about the needs of the show and everyone involved in it. That includes the actors, the crew, and the audience.

Go out into the house and sit in several places. Make sure you sit in the worst seats—usually the end seats in the first and last rows. If your theater has seating in odd places, sit in those as well. Take note of how much of the stage—and what parts—you can see from each place. This gives you an idea of how the stage will have to be set up. You want the audience to have a good view of the performance—but no view of anything going on backstage!

Now, go backstage. Does your theater have dressing rooms, or will you need to set some up? How long does it take to walk from the dressing room? During the show, you will have actors popping on and off the stage. Crew members will be hovering in the wings, ready to dash on for scene changes. The backstage area will be crammed with stuff—sets and equipment needed to move those sets, as well as costumes and props.

Figure out where all this stuff will go. You will want the prop table near the stage. Actors can grab what they need right before they go onstage and put it back as soon as they get off. Your prop table must be large enough to fit everything, and it must be easy to reach. However, it shouldn't be placed so that people are likely to bump into it. To make this process go a bit more smoothly, you might want to recruit someone to be the prop master, a crew member whose job it is to find the props and keep them organized before, during, and after each performance.

Sometimes, a costume change must happen so fast that the actress has no time to go back to the dressing room. This means you

The Stage Manager's Toolkit

Carpenters wear tool belts, doctors carry black bags, and moms haul around big purses. As stage manager, you will join the ranks of people who need access to stuff.

Lots of situations come up during a show. Sometimes, they may be minor emergencies! The actors and the crew spend long hours rehearsing. There isn't always time to go get the things they need. A stage manager can become everyone's best friend just by having a few of life's little necessities on hand. Put together a kit with a few basics. You might include tissues, bandages, wet wipes, and hand sanitizer. Toss in some gum and mints, a phone book, and change for the drink machine. You should probably avoid adding any types of medicine. Many schools have strict rules against sharing medication.

need a quick-change area in the wings. It won't be as well-equipped as a dressing room, but it must meet some minimum standards in terms of privacy and enough room to change clothes. You may need more than one quick-change area—for example, one for boys and one for girls.

Looking for Clues

So what's your first task, after signing on to be stage manager? Is it making sure your headset has fresh batteries? Investing in a good pair of walking shoes? Those things should be done, but not yet.

Before you do anything at the theater, you should go home and read the script. Listen to recordings of the songs. Get to know that musical like it's your own family history.

Reading the script and listening to the songs are the first steps in staging a musical. Knowing the story and music thoroughly will help the stage manager do her job.

The first time you sit down with the script, read it straight through and simply enjoy it. Try to remember the feelings it gives you. Later on, you will have rehearsed each scene so many times that you may forget about the big picture. That's when you need to remind yourself what the story is actually about. When everyone else is stressing about which hand to carry a glass in, you can remind them that it doesn't make a lot of difference—the audience should be caught up in the story.

Once you've read the script for enjoyment, it's time to get to work. What happens in the show that you will be responsible for? Many things happen onstage that the actors don't control. Lighting, sound, and special effects depend on the crew. They wait for the signal (the cue) from the stage manager.

Read the play again. This time, think of it as a scavenger hunt. You're looking for cue clues. Suppose a stage direction reads, "Elizabeth crosses the room and answers the door." You can assume that someone knocked at the door or rang the doorbell. That's a sound effect, and the stage manager may need to handle it.

However, the script may not spell out the stage directions. They might be implied only. Suppose the hero and heroine are out for a walk. The heroine exclaims, "This rain will ruin my dress!" We know then that a rainstorm has started. You may need to cue a thunderclap, a flash of lightning, or a lighting effect that looks like rain.

Familiarize yourself with other details about the play. Learn about the places and customs. This information can help the actors and the technical crew. If there are foreign words in the script, learn how to pronounce them. If there are references to people or events, find out how they relate. It is not absolutely necessary for the stage manager of a musical to be able to read music, but being able to follow a score can be a bonus if cues happen during an orchestration.

Put It in Writing

Here's a stage management joke: "How many stage managers does it take to change a lightbulb?" Answer: "One. And it's on my list."

One of the stage manager's main jobs is to keep everything organized. He will check in with people again and again to be sure everyone is informed and on schedule. And he will write it all

Important notices about rehearsals or other meetings are posted on the callboard. Actors should get in the habit of checking it regularly.

down. This involves a lot of paper. It helps if people can read your handwriting.

The actors are cast. The crew is assembled. Now, it's time to make up a contact sheet. This lists everyone involved with the show and how they can be reached. Include their home phone numbers, cell phone numbers, e-mail addresses, street addresses, and any other important information. You probably won't need their locker numbers or where they'll be during fourth period. However, if you think it will help, put it in! Give the list to everyone in the show. Musicals require a lot of people doing different things, at different times, and in different places. A contact sheet will help everyone stay in touch.

The stage manager also keeps the callboard. Think of this as a newsletter for the company. The callboard will generally be a bulletin board located near the theater. On it, the stage manager will post information about rehearsal schedules, meetings, or any other news about the show. Tell your cast and crew to get in the habit of checking it each time they come to the theater.

Staying Safe and Sane

Theater people are dedicated. They are often willing to do just about anything for a show. Sometimes, there is a lot of pressure to get things done on time. They might feel they need to save money. It may be tempting to cut corners.

A stage manager should keep a close eye on the safety of everyone involved. This could mean making sure that people using tools are wearing safety goggles. It might mean not letting anyone climb too high on a ladder without being in a harness. It means making sure the stage crew has the right equipment to safely move

Bright lights and big sounds depend on a maze of twisty little wires. Before each performance, the stage manager will check to see that everything is working properly.

sets. It also means organizing the backstage area. Sets, equipment, and props should all have definite places.

Before each performance, a stage manager should check the lights and sound system to make sure they are working properly. Then, he walks the stage and checks the sets. He does whatever the actors do: dance on the table, walk up the stairs, lean over the balcony. If anything seems creaky or unsteady, he alerts the director or the adult who is in charge of the sets.

As stage manager, you need your own space backstage. Set up a desk, table, or podium that is just for you. Here is where you can keep all the stuff you will need. Include a flashlight (or two), spike tape, pencils, paper, a tape measure, and a calculator.

During performances, dress like a member of the stage crew. Wear black or dark clothing and shoes that are comfortable and quiet. Keep a low profile with your clothes. If you call the show from the wings, it's possible that you could be visible during a scene change. And who knows—if someone in the crew doesn't show up, you might have to fill in!

Rehearsals

When we talk about long, difficult rehearsals, it's usually the actors who get our sympathy. But the stage manager has it just as bad. The nitty-gritty part of the stage manager's job starts with rehearsals.

Let's Run It Again

It takes a lot of hours of practice to put on a musical. Things go wrong, and wrong again. But eventually, it comes together. Each rehearsal builds on the ones before it until the show starts to look like a show.

One of the first rehearsals will probably be a read-through. That's just what it sounds like. Actors simply read through the script. They can experiment with how to deliver their lines. Next come rehearsals for blocking, which is how the actors move onstage. There may also be special rehearsals for singing, dancing, and special scenes (such as a fight). A run-through is when the actors perform part of the show (or the whole thing) without stopping. Technical aspects are usually not included in a run-through. Early run-throughs are sometimes called "stagger-throughs" because everyone is still figuring out what to do.

A dress parade isn't exactly a rehearsal. It's more like a fashion show. The actors wear their costumes onstage to show how they look under the lights. Then come technical rehearsals, when the

Actors use their scripts at the beginning of the rehearsal process, but at some point, they will have to give them up! The stage manager will need to prompt lines if actors forget their lines.

crew adds lights, sounds, and special effects. Finally, the whole musical is staged in a full dress rehearsal.

One of the stage manager's jobs is to time each scene, as well as the entire performance. It's also important to know how much time there is between scenes so that he can plan set changes.

About halfway through the rehearsal process, the actors stop using their scripts. However, they may have come to depend on them to remember their lines. The first "off book" rehearsals can be rough. The stage manager may need to prompt lines. Check with the director about how he or she wants to handle this. Some directors will pause to give the actor time to remember the line. Others will tell the actors to call "line" as soon as they need it so that they don't interrupt the flow. When an actor calls "line," the prompter should read the first few words of it immediately. Don't try to "act" the line—just say it and let the actor take over.

Professional stage managers watch the rehearsals and write daily reports. This is not usually necessary in high school. However, it's a good skill to practice if you are interested in stage management as a career.

Blocking

Let's say your musical has a cast of fifty people. You have two leads and five supporting characters. There are ten more bit parts and the chorus. All these people have to speak their lines, sing, dance, and move around.

The director and choreographer figure out how all the movements will fit together. This process is called blocking. The term probably originates from Victorian times. Back then, directors worked with a miniature set and used wooden blocks to represent the actors.

Headset Etiquette

Can you hear me now? On a headset, anything you say can be heard by everyone else. Sometimes, this can get annoying. Worse, sometimes things are said that should have been private.

Use the headset only for things that are necessary to the show. If you are up in the booth and a crew member is in the flies, you need the headset to tell him when to begin lowering a piece of scenery. But if you're discussing whether or not to have pepperoni or mushrooms on your pizza, that conversation can wait until you meet up in person.

Tempers can run short on a show. People are spending long hours together, and it becomes easy to obsess on what other people are doing—especially what they are doing wrong. Do not use the headset to gossip or criticize others. It won't help to create a spirit of goodwill.

It's the stage manager's job to remember what the director decides and to write it down in the script. (It's also smart to have the actors record their blocking movements on their own scripts.)

The director may say something like, "Claire, I want you farther upstage when you finish that line." Claire will walk a few steps upstage until the director says, "Good. Right there." Or, she may say, "Josh, when you finish the number with the rest of the mechanics, jump off the car while Claire is still walking. And the rest of you—mechanics!—you freeze when Josh lands. Let him take three steps toward Claire and then fall back into the line just as the song ends."

Stage manager, hope you're paying attention, with your pencil—not pen!—at the ready. You need to record all this, either on a diagram of the stage or using blocking notation. (See page 35 for an example.)

After blocking, the stage manager must spike (tape) the set. He will indicate where the set pieces will be placed. Sometimes, he might also mark some of the actors' positions. It might be helpful to use different colors of spike tape in order to keep pieces organized.

Stage Directions

The stage is a big place. To deal with it easily, break it down into sections. Think of the stage as a tic-tac-toe board. There will be upstage, downstage, and midstage. In the other direction, there are left, right, and center. You can abbreviate each part. For example, "UR" will mean "upper right," and "MC" will mean "midstage center." If the musical is particularly complicated, you may have to divide up your stage into even smaller areas.

Blocking notation is a shorthand that shows where actors move and when. For example, on a diagram of the stage, you might use the characters' initials, with arrows pointing to where they will move. On a script, you might circle a word and write "C. walks UR" (Claire begins walking upstage right) and then circle another word and write "C. stops table" (Claire stops at the table). Each stage manager has a different approach for this, but it should be clear and consistent. Find a way that works for you.

On Cue

The stage manager controls the technical parts of the show, such as lights, sound, and special effects. During a performance, he

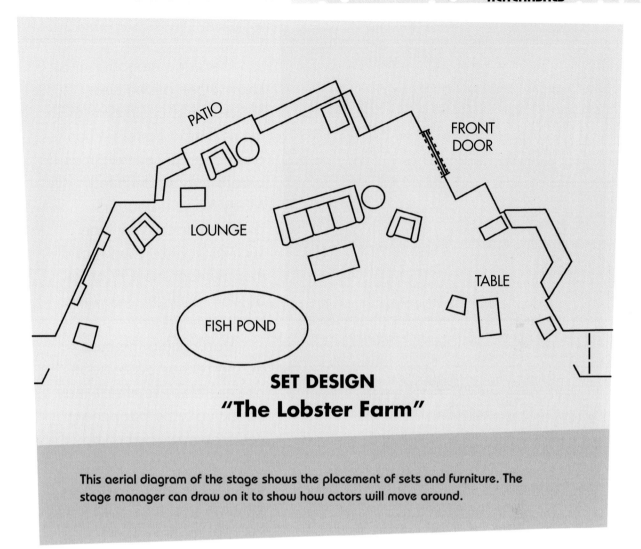

**SET DESIGN
"The Lobster Farm"**

This aerial diagram of the stage shows the placement of sets and furniture. The stage manager can draw on it to show how actors will move around.

"calls" these cues. He announces when it's time for them so that the technicians can make them happen.

There are different kinds of cues. A text cue comes from the lines in the script. A musical cue will be in the score. A visual cue means the stage manager takes his signal from the action onstage. Occasionally, a cue will not have an obvious signal. In those cases, the stage manager can time it from something that happens before. For example, a gunshot might come three seconds after an actor walks offstage.

A podium in the wings gives the stage manager a good view of the stage while she calls the show.

The stage manager must know when all the cues happen and make note of them. (Use a pencil—cues often change several times before they're definite.) Many stage managers divide their cues by type, such as light or sound, and then number them in order. So, the first light cue would be "Lights 1."

Start calling the cues during rehearsals as soon as possible. The effects may not actually be happening yet. However, by calling them, you get everybody used to the idea of where they are and how long they last. Try to make them realistic. Suppose it takes several seconds for the lights to dim and then go dark. Instead of just saying "Lights out," say, "Lights coming down . . . down . . . and out." During this time, if an actor has to hold a position or the final note of a song, it will get him used to the length of time.

Some stage managers like to re-create sound effects as well. If a phone is ringing, you could just say, "Phone rings." But it is more realistic to ring an actual phone. Or, you could make a ringing sound yourself. Anything you do to make it seem like an actual performance will help the company—and that's your job.

The Prompt Book

The title of this book gets capital letters: the Prompt Book. You know those adventure movies where the hero faces all kinds of impossible situations, but above all, he must hold on to the treasure? In a musical, the prompt book is the treasure. It is the doorway to knowledge and the key to understanding. And the stage manager has to write it.

Every detail related to the production of a play or musical goes into the stage manager's prompt book.

The prompt book includes a copy of the script, with lots of room on every page to make notes. If you use a thick, three-ring notebook, it will be easy to add or remove pages. During rehearsals, the stage manager will make notes on the script about things that happen. For example, you might write blocking movements on one side of the page. On the other side, you will record the cues for lights, sounds, and special effects. (You're using a pencil, right? Things are going to change.)

The prompt book should also include all the other things a stage manager keeps track of. The stage manager knows who's onstage in every scene. He knows what they're wearing, what they're carrying, and when they make their exits. He knows which crew members handle which scene changes. The stage manager tracks everything using a chart called a plot. There will be costume plots, shift plots, etc. Just like in a story, the plot outlines everything needed to reach a specific goal.

By the end of rehearsals, the notebook will probably be bulging. It will hold every scrap of information related to the show.

In *Stage Management: A Guidebook of Practical Techniques*, Lawrence Stern wrote, "No critic will ever review your prompt book. Great paperwork does not necessarily make great theater." Certainly, messy stage managers have managed great plays. However, neatness does count. If the stage manager misses a show, somebody must step in to do his job. The prompt book is the instruction manual. A well-kept prompt book should be clear enough that someone who is looking at it for the first time could call the show correctly.

Tech Week

The week before opening night brings a lot of nervousness. This is tech week, and it's when all the technical aspects of the show are added.

Traditionally, technical rehearsals run for hours. The actors do a lot of standing around while the lighting and sound people try to fix problems. Usually, there is a series of technical rehearsals, and the stage manager is in charge.

The first step is a paper tech. The technical heads (sound, lighting, effects) meet off stage with the stage manager and make sure everyone knows what is supposed to happen. A dry tech moves everyone to the stage, but the actors get to stay home. Only the

Will it work? During technical rehearsals, crew members finally get to take the stage and finalize the details of sound, lighting, and special effects.

technical stuff is practiced. A cue to cue (sometimes written as Q2Q) fast-forwards through the show, skipping most of the performing in between. The actors are there, but to save time, they perform only the little bits before the technical cues.

The crew also needs to practice their set changes. Complicated changes may first be done with the lights on, in slow motion,

Two hands on the board: crew members need a good sense of timing as they listen for cues and then carry them out.

without actors in the way. Next, they add the actors' exits and rev it up to half speed. Then, they go to full speed, using the same low lighting that they will have during the performance. The stage manager should develop plots to show who will move sets or objects, and how. He will be in charge of assigning people to the running crew (the people who work during the performance).

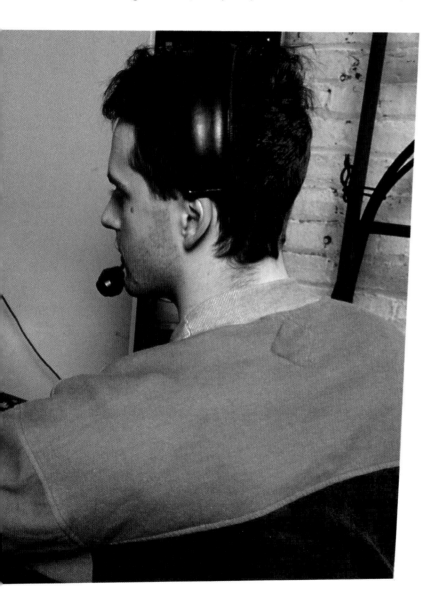

Think you have everything figured out? Now, it's time for the full dress rehearsal, which includes all props, costumes, set changes, and effects.

It would be a rare show where everything went right the first time. The point of tech rehearsals is to work out the kinks. The actors weren't perfect the first time out, and the crew won't be either. Don't be afraid to experiment. If a set won't move off one way, try it another.

Finally, let the crew practice. They will get smoother and faster as they get the hang of it.

Tech week can be exhausting, but the effort should be worth it. By the time opening night comes, you'll know exactly how everything works, and you'll feel comfortable that everyone knows what to do.

From Curtain to Curtain

On performance nights, the stage manager will spend most of his time calling the show, either from a booth overlooking the stage or from the wings. Before that, he will check to make sure the stage, sets, and cast and crew are ready.

Thirty minutes before curtain time, the stage manager usually calls "half-hour" to the actors. He will give additional warnings at fifteen minutes, ten minutes (this is also the time for "crew to places"), and five minutes. At two minutes, he calls "places." He always says "please," and the actors always say "thank you." It's important that the actors answer. That's how the stage manager knows they heard him!

Calling the Show

Actors will tell you there's more to saying a line than just saying it. A good actor delivers his line.

As stage manager, your lines may not be as colorful as the actors', but they are just as important. And just like theirs, your lines will be most effective if they are delivered in a certain way. In rehearsals, practice calling cues so that everyone gets used to how you do it. Then, during performances, everyone will feel comfortable with the process.

Armed with tape, a notebook, and a headset, the stage manager is ready to tackle whatever problem arises.

Lawrence Stern wrote in *Stage Management*: "The new stage manager may be compared to a person just learning to drive a car; she or he is afraid to step on the gas pedal. The experienced stage manager, on the other hand, gives her or his cues with the authority of a marine drill sergeant, but in a whisper."

About a minute before the cue is supposed to happen, the

stage manager calls a warning with the name and number of the cue like this: "Warning, lights 12." The lighting technician responds with "Lights warned." When it's time for the lights, the stage manager will say, "Lights 12 . . . go." That "go" means it is time for the cue. The lighting person should have his finger hovering over the button, but he should not push it until the word "go." The stage manager must anticipate this moment and say the word just a split second before the cue is actually supposed to happen. Sometimes, two or more cues happen together. So, you might say, "Lights 27, sound 9, and effects 2 together . . . go."

You could think of stage managing as being like driving. You are driving the show, and the prompt book is your driver's education manual. However, if you have ever driven a car, you know that it's more important to look at the road than the book. When you're stage managing a show, you should not have your nose in the book—you should be watching the stage. The prompt book is only a model of the show. If an actor moves early or a light comes up late, it's not going to say so in the book. The actual show is happening on the stage. That's what you have to respond to.

Rehearsals have gone perfectly. Everyone knows their job and is doing it properly and consistently. But guess what? It doesn't last. Mistakes are bound to happen. In these situations, your job gets harder. The first thing you have to do is actually a "don't": don't panic. The mistake is there; it's happened. You can't take it back. Getting flustered isn't going to help. Getting angry isn't going to help. So, stay focused on what's going on. Think about how you can fix the problem, or at least minimize the damage. In many cases, the best plan is to simply move on. Once the performance has finished, do what you can to make sure it doesn't happen again.

Audience Participation

A show is almost like a living thing. It all happens in real time, and it may be changed by any little thing—a dancer's misstep, an actor's sudden sneeze, a sound man who pushes the "doorbell" button instead of the "phone ringing" button.

The audience will never see the stage manager's hard work, but they will notice if it doesn't get done!

In general, however, the cast and crew know what to do. They do it correctly most of the time. By the time rehearsals are finished, the performance feels comfortable.

And then the audience comes.

It's tempting to think, "Who are these people, and what are they doing at my show?" Then, you remember: they're the whole reason for the show in the first place. Theater does not really become theater until someone is watching.

The audience is a powerful force. They may laugh at the wrong moments. They may not laugh at the right moments. One of them might have a sudden sneeze, disturbing a solemn moment. Their laughter or clapping might be so loud, the crew can't hear you give an instruction. You just never know.

Actors gain experience working with—or around—the audience's reaction. However, occasionally the stage manager has to adjust, too. For example, the audience might clap longer than you expected after a song. In that case, you might delay bringing the lights down because it's clear the audience wants just a few more moments of absorbing the scene.

You don't want to change too much, or it will confuse the cast and crew. But you don't want to ignore your audience either.

Dealing with Disasters

You've heard it before: the show must go on.

Actually, it doesn't. That's the goal, of course. It would be good if the show went on, even when something goes wrong. And usually, that's the case. A missed cue, a flubbed line, a lost prop— none of those is a big deal. Then, you have medium-sized problems. Maybe the spotlight stops working, the sound system

Ritual Behavior

Every show is different—at least onstage. But behind the stage, theater people like to keep some things the same. Theater is filled with traditions and superstitions. For example, no one should whistle backstage. Centuries ago (before headsets), crew members used to whistle to signal each other. Random whistling could cause problems, so the "no whistling" rule continues to this day. It's bad luck to say "good luck"—that's why actors are told to "break a leg" instead. And unless you are performing Shakespeare's *Macbeth*, do not dare to breathe the name of that play. Throughout history, this show has been plagued with bad luck, so theater folk agree to not even mention its name.

On Broadway, the chorus member with the most credits wears the gypsy robe. This robe is decorated with art from recent shows. The wearer circles the stage three times counterclockwise and lets other cast members touch the robe for good luck. The youngest person ever to wear the robe was only twelve years old!

dies, or a set piece collapses. Even these can be overcome. Actors can ad-lib to make up for a missed cue or even a missing set. On her Web site Stage Managers Do Make Coffee, stage manager Carissa Dollar writes about a show she worked on. The stage lights failed in the middle of the performance. The cast ad-libbed as the crew turned on the work lights. Everyone finished the performance using just the work lights. "The audience laughed and clapped just as hard at the end of the performance," Dollar wrote. "The cast was impressed with how quickly the crew solved the problem."

It's a good idea to have a plan in place for understudies as well. Sometimes, you might have a day's notice to replace a lead.

At the other extreme, you might have the lead come down with stomach flu in act 1. You need a replacement by act 2. This is when the stage manager is tested to the limit. This is when she has to be creative and flexible under pressure.

But sometimes, a problem is simply too big. In these cases, it's often a question of safety. In professional productions, it is the stage manager's job to stop the show if necessary. In high school, you will probably have an adult who can make this call. However, if you spot an immediate danger, step in. The show may still go on—after a slight delay.

Keep It Up and Take It Down

In professional productions, the director's job is finished when opening night arrives. He has crafted the show. Now, he turns the reins over to the stage manager. The stage manager is now the boss. The stage manager has worked closely with the director throughout rehearsals. He understands what the director wants for the show. Actors sometimes get bored doing the same show over and over. They may become "creative" with their lines or movements. The crew might get a little lazy. It's the stage manager's job to maintain the show. He makes sure the company continues to deliver the same quality show, night after night. After all, the audience who comes on the one hundredth night is still paying the same rate that people did on opening night.

In high school shows, however, the director stays throughout the show. Maintenance isn't too much of an issue. Most shows run for only a couple of weekends. There isn't that much time for things to fall apart. Nonetheless, the stage manager should still pay attention. If the director is not aware of a problem, the stage manager can let him know.

Crew members work with the stage manager to determine how sets will be carried on and off the stage. Just like actors, the crew may need a little rehearsal to get their entrances and exits perfect.

At the end of the run, everything has to come down. The "strike" is rarely anyone's favorite job. All the excitement has passed. All that remains is work. It can be draining, both physically and emotionally. Striking the set is a very real reminder that the show has ended. Over the last few weeks or months, the cast and crew may have become like family. Now, it's time to say goodbye.

The strike may be scheduled for immediately after the final performance. If that is the case, try to make sure that no cast parties or other events are planned for the same time. That way, the strike crew won't miss anything. If they know they have time to get everything done, they are less likely to hurry through the job. Then, they won't end up damaging the sets or hurting themselves.

Finally, be sure to return any props or costumes that were borrowed. Check to see that set pieces are stored properly. Clean up the stage, the dressing rooms, and any other areas you used. In short, make sure everything is left in order.

After High School

Stage managing includes many duties. There is a high level of responsibility. Most high school students will not have the time to do everything a professional stage manager would. They also may not have authority over other students. They may not be involved in auditions or talks about the budget. They probably won't set schedules or manage rehearsals.

However, high school stage managers can get involved in areas that professionals do not. For example, they can learn about publicity and house management—things they can draw on if they decide on a professional career.

Many professional stage managers are members of a union like the Actors' Equity Association (AEA). Membership has both

A few minutes before curtain, backstage can be a frantic place. Keeping good notes throughout rehearsals will help make last-minute checks easier.

advantages and disadvantages. Members get the support of the union on things like how much they get paid or how many hours they have to work. However, once a stage manager joins the AEA, he can't work in a non-equity theater. This might not be a problem in New York or Los Angeles, where there are many theaters. However, in smaller cities, he might have a tough time finding a job.

If you are interested in stage management as a career, some colleges teach it. However, even more than other types of jobs, stage managers learn by doing. There is no substitute for being backstage, with your clipboard in hand.

Even if you have learned everything you should do, you still have to do it.

High school is a good place to start.

The lights are down. You can hear the murmur of the audience, waiting for the curtain. And you know, even though you are not onstage, that your performance is vital to the show.

blocking The process of determining how actors move on the stage.

callboard A place to post information about the show for the cast and crew.

company The cast, crew, and staff; everyone involved in putting on a particular show.

concierge A person who helps other people get information or organize activities.

contact sheet A list of people involved with a show and how to reach them.

cue A signal to indicate a technical effect in a show.

dress parade When performers wear their costumes onstage to check how they look.

dry tech A technical rehearsal without the actors.

flies The upper workings of a theater, from where scenery is lowered and lifted.

off book The point in rehearsals when actors stop using their scripts.

paper tech A meeting where the technical people organize all the technical cues.

places An instruction given by the stage manager indicating that cast and crew should take their opening positions to start the show.

plot A chart that gives information about a specific aspect of a show.

pre-production Refers to the time before rehearsals begin and the tasks that must be accomplished then.

prompt To say a few words of an actor's line in order to help him remember.

prop Short for "property"; a physical object used in a show.

quick-change A costume change that must be done quickly, usually without returning to the dressing room.

read-through A rehearsal where the actors read through the script without moving around.

run The number of performances scheduled for a show.

running crew The crew members who operate, or "run," an actual performance.

spike To tape the stage to indicate positions of sets or actor movements.

stage direction A written note in the script that indicates an action.

strike To take down the set after the run of a show.

understudy An actor who performs a role if the main actor cannot perform.

Actors' Equity Association

National Office
165 West 46th Street
New York, NY 10036
(212) 869-8530
Web site: http://www.actorsequity.org
A labor union for actors and stage managers, the AEA promotes theater
as a part of society and focuses on improving working conditions for
its members.

Canadian Actors Equity Association

44 Victoria Street, 12th Floor
Toronto, ON M5C 3C4
Canada
(416) 867-9165
E-mail: info@caea.com
Web site: http://www.caea.com
A labor union representing performers, directors, and stage managers,
this organization focuses on improving working conditions and
supporting live theater in Canada.

Canadian Institute for Theatre Technology

340-207 Bank Street
Ottawa, ON K2P 2N2
Canada
(613) 482-1165 or (888) 271-3383
E-mail: info@citt.org
Web site: http://www.citt.org

This organization helps its members through education and professional development, and promotes live performance in Canada.

Educational Theatre Association

2343 Auburn Avenue
Cincinnati, OH 45219
(513) 421-3900
E-mail: info@edta.org
Web site: http://www.edta.org
The Educational Theatre Association works with students and teachers from middle school through college to support theater education.

The Stage Managers' Association

P.O. Box 275, Times Square Station
New York, NY 10108-0275
(212) 691-5633
E-mail: info@stagemanagers.org
Web site: http://www.stagemanagers.org
The stage managers in this professional organization share problems and ideas, and work to educate each other.

Theatre Ontario

215 Spadina Avenue, Suite 210
Toronto, ON M5T 2C7
Canada
(416) 408-4556
E-mail: info@theatreontario.org
Web site: http://www.theatreontario.org
Theatre Ontario promotes high-quality theater in the province by offering training programs and resources, and working with the government.

U.S. Institute for Theatre Technology, Inc. (USITT)

315 South Crouse Avenue, Suite 200
Syracuse, NY 13210
(315) 463-6463 or (800) 938-7488
E-mail: info@office.usitt.org
Web site: http://www.usitt.org/index.html
The USITT promotes education and communication among people
    working in performing arts design and technology.

Web Sites

Due to the changing nature of Internet links, Rosen Publishing has
developed an online list of Web sites related to the subject of this
book. This site is updated regularly. Please use this link to access
the list:

http://www.rosenlinks.com/hsm/stma

FOR FURTHER READING

Campbell, Drew. *Technical Theater for Nontechnical People*. New York, NY: Allworth Press, 2004.

Friedman, Lise. *Break a Leg! The Kid's Guide to Acting and Stagecraft*. New York, NY: Workman Publishing Company, 2002.

Ionazzi, Daniel A. *The Stage Management Handbook*. Crozet, VA: Betterway Publications, Inc., 1992.

Lawler, Mike. *Careers in Technical Theater*. New York, NY: Allworth Press, 2007.

Novak, Elaine A., and Deborah Novak. *Staging Musical Theatre*. Cincinnati, OH: Betterway Books, 1996.

White, Matthew. *Staging a Musical*. New York, NY: Theatre Arts Books/Routledge, 1999.

Apperson, Linda. *Stage Managing and Theatre Etiquette*. Chicago, IL: Ivan R. Dee, 1998.

CNN.com. "Stage manager: 'Never been the same.'" October 10, 2001. Retrieved June 26, 2008 (http://archives.cnn.com/2001/CAREER/dayonthejob/08/01/stage.manager/index.html).

Copley, Soozie, and Philippa Killner. *Stage Management*. Ramsbury, England: The Crowood Press, Ltd., 2001.

Dollar, Carissa. "Stage Managers Do Make Coffee: A Handbook for Stage Managers." February 7, 2000. Retrieved July 8, 2008 (http://www.geocities.com/dollariquestnet/SMhandbook.html).

Fazio, Larry. *Stage Manager: The Professional Experience*. Woburn, MA: Focal Press, 2000.

Howard, Chelsea. "A Day in the Life of: A Stage Manager." BGNews.com, March 3, 2006. Retrieved June 25, 2008 (http://media.www.bgnews.com/media/storage/paper883/news/2006/03/03/Pulse/A.Day.In.The.Life.Of.A.Stage.Manager-1653498.shtml).

Kaluta, John. *The Perfect Stage Crew*. New York, NY: Allworth Press, 2003.

Kenrick, John. *The Complete Idiot's Guide to Amateur Theatricals*. New York, NY: Penguin Group, Inc., 2006.

Lawler, Mike. "Responsible for Everything." *Dramatics*, October 2005.

McGinnis, Dave. "Do It Right, or Do It Elsewhere." Stage-Directions.com, April 4, 2008. Retrieved June 24, 2008 (http://stage-directions.com/index.php?option=com_content&task=view&id=732&Itemid=75).

Pincus-Roth, Zachary. "Ask Playbill.com: Stage Managers." Playbill. com, November 2, 2007. Retrieved June 26, 2008 (http:// www.playbill.com/features/article/112488.html).

Pollick, Michael. "What Does a Stage Manager Do?" Wisegeek. com. Retrieved June 26, 2008 (http://www.wisegeek.com/ what-does-a-stage-manager-do.htm).

Rothstein, Mervyn. "A Life in the Theatre: Production Stage Manager and Associate Director Peter Lawrence." Playbill.com, February 17, 2006. Retrieved June 25, 2008 (http://www. playbill.com/features/article/98021.html).

Schneider, Doris. *The Art and Craft of Stage Management.* Fort Worth, TX: Harcourt Brace & Company, 1997.

Schumacher, Thomas, and Jeff Kurtti. *How Does the Show Go On?* New York, NY: Disney Editions, 2007.

Stern, Lawrence. *Stage Management: A Guidebook of Practical Techniques.* Newton, MA: Allyn and Bacon, Inc., 1987.

UpstageReview.org. "Defining Stage Management." Retrieved June 26, 2008 (http://upstagereview.org/Misc%20Tech% 20Articles/definingsm.pdf).

About the Author

Diane Bailey acted and sang in several of her high school's musicals. She never had the lead, so she spent a lot of time hanging out with the stage crew. Since then, she has always found backstage to be just as much fun as onstage. Bailey has two children and writes on a variety of nonfiction topics.

Photo Credits

Cover (background), p. 1 Sisse Brimberg & Cotton Coulson/Reportage/Getty Images; cover (inset) © www.istockphoto.com/espion; pp. 4–5 © Gary Hershorn/Reuters/Corbis; p. 8 Ryan McVay/Lifesize/Getty Images; pp. 9, 10, 11, 12, 19, 26, 31, 36, 37 © Michael McGarty; p. 16 © Jeff Greenberg/The Image Works; pp. 20–21 Loungepark/The Image Bank/Getty Images; p 24 Shutterstock.com; p. 28 Martien Mulder/Stone/Getty Images; p. 39 © Syracuse Newspapers/Michelle Gabel/The Image Works; pp. 40–41 © Cathy Melloan Resources/PhotoEdit; pp. 44–45 Digital Vision/Getty Images; p. 47 Rod Morata/Stone+/Getty Images; pp. 51, 53 © Jeff Greenberg/PhotoEdit.

Designer: Sam Zavieh; Editor: Bethany Bryan
Photo Researcher: Cindy Reiman